North American Birds

HOW TO USE THIS BOOK

Read about birds and their habitats in the eight-page booklet and choose stickers from the sticker spreads to fill in the scenes.

•

Don't forget that your stickers can be stuck down and peeled off again. If you are careful, you can use your bird stickers more than once.

•

You can also use these stickers to decorate your own books and notes, or for project work at school.

Written and edited by Elizabeth Hester
Designed by Melissa Chung
Jacket designed by Tai Blanche

Publisher Chuck Lang • **Creative Director** Tina Vaughan
Managing Editor Beth Sutinis • **Managing Art Editor** Michelle Baxter
Jacket Art Director Dirk Kaufman • **Production** Chris Avgherinos

First Edition, 2003
Second Edition, 2005

21 22
022-ND084-Oct/2005

Published in the United States by DK Publishing
1450 Broadway, Suite 801, New York, NY 10018

ISBN-13: 978-0-7566-1509-3

Printed and bound in China

DK Publishing would like to thank:
Southern Lights Custom Publishing

Photographs used with the permission of:
Fred Alsop, Ron Austing, Dennis Avon, Mike Danzenbaker, Mike Dunning, Frank Greenaway,
Kevin T. Karlson, Cyril Laubscher, S. Mazlowski, Brian E. Small, Tom Vezo, and CORBIS

A WORLD OF IDEAS:
SEE ALL THERE IS TO KNOW

www.dk.com

At the park

With wide open spaces for flying, grass to look for seeds in, and lots of trees and bushes, a city park is just the spot for birds to build a home—even in the middle of a city. Grassy parks and backyards are full of interesting birds. Just look to the trees to do some great birdwatching close to home.

Tufted Titmouse
A Titmouse will sometimes hang upside-down from a tree branch while looking around for food.

Northern Cardinal
The "Redbird" is the official bird of seven states: Illinois, Indiana, Kentucky, North Carolina, Ohio, Virginia, and West Virginia.

Downy Woodpecker
Each fall, a Downy Woodpecker makes a new home by pecking into a tree trunk. It can take eight days to dig out a new roost.

Carolina Chickadee
Chickadees love eating sunflower seeds. They will also snack on insects, moths, and berries.

At the seashore

A seascape is the perfect place for birds who love fishing over open water, nesting in a rocky perch, or strutting through sandy dunes. Some shore birds prefer one coast over another, while others can be seen in lots of different regions. You can pretend this beach is anywhere at all.

Sanderling
This little bird runs back and forth on the beach, looking for sand crabs as they wash ashore.

Laughing Gull
This gull's call sounds like laughter. Laughing Gulls sometimes steal food right out of a Brown Pelican's pouch!

Atlantic Puffin
Puffins build their nests in burrows on the shore. Their strong wings let them fly in the air and swim underwater.

Black Oystercatcher
The Oystercatcher uses its long, chisel-like beak to pry open the shells of its food.

Brown Pelican
The Brown Pelican flies over the water, then dives down to scoop up fish with the large pouch in its beak.

Mountain and Woodland Birds

American Redstart
Lives mainly in forests, but winters in the tropics

Sharp-shinned Hawk
Lives in pine forests, but migrates through many habitats

Baltimore Oriole
Lives in woods, neighborhoods, and trees near streams

Eastern Phoebe
Lives in open woods near streams or other water

Golden Eagle
Lives on mountains and other rugged places

Black-and-white Warbler
Lives in woods and forests

Song Sparrow
Especially likes brushy areas near water

Blue-gray Gnatcatcher
Lives in various kinds of woods

Blue-headed Vireo
Lives in woods or in trees along streams

Vermillion Flycatcher
Lives in trees near water sources

Ruby-crowned Kinglet
Lives in forests and wooded yards

American Kestrel
Lives near woods or in wooded canyons

Scarlet Tanager
Stays mainly at the tops of tall trees in the woods

Pileated Woodpecker
Lives in forests, swamps, woods, and cities

Rufous Hummingbird
Lives in woodlands, meadows, and mountains

Belted Kingfisher
Found wherever there is water

Peregrine Falcon
Nests on cliffs or on buildings in big cities

Park and Backyard Birds

Killdeer
Lives mainly
on riverbanks

House Sparrow
Lives in cities,
towns, yards,
farms,
and ranches

Eastern Screech-Owl
Lives in wooded lots
and in gardens

American Crow
Lives anywhere
there are trees

Yellow Warbler
Lives near thickets,
willows, alders,
creeks, streams,
swamps, and in
neighborhoods

Northern Bobwhite
Lives in farmlands,
grasslands, open
forests, and
open country

Northern Cardinal
Lives in thickets, parks,
gardens, and yards

Carolina Chickadee
Lives in
woods and
neighborhoods

Mourning Dove
Lives in cities,
towns, and open
country

Red-bellied Woodpecker
Lives in swamps,
woods, and
neighborhoods

Ruby-throated Hummingbird
Lives in gardens,
backyards, and near
the forest edge

Downy Woodpecker
Lives anywhere
there are trees,
including
suburbs and
orchards

Tufted Titmouse
Lives in damp
woods, parks,
and neighborhoods

Yellow-rumped Warbler
Lives in woods,
forests, and
wooded yards

Painted Bunting
Lives in thickets, hedgerows,
and briar patches

Seashore, Lake, and River Birds

Sanderling
Lives on rocky or sandy seashores

Semipalmated Plover
Lives near beaches, lakes, and rivers

American White Pelican
Lives on western lakes in the summer and in southwestern and Gulf Coast states in the winter

Willet
Lives on sandy seashores or in freshwater marshes

Brown Pelican
Lives near sandy beaches on the southern coasts

Laughing Gull
Lives on beaches, salt marshes, and bays

Black Oystercatcher
Lives along the Pacific coast

Great Egret
Lives near freshwater ponds, saltwater marshes, and along the coast

White-faced Ibis
Lives near marshes and on the coast

Common Tern
Lives along beaches, lakes, and rivers

Atlantic Puffin
Lives on the Atlantic coast

Osprey
Lives on coasts, rivers, and lakes

Bald Eagle
Lives on the coast and by large lakes

Common Loon
Lives on the ocean or coast in the winter, and by lakes and rivers near forests in the summer

Herring Gull
Lives near coasts, harbors, garbage dumps, rivers, and lakes

Swamp and Wetland Birds

Green Heron
Lives near swamps, ponds, and wooded streams

Cinnamon Teal
Lives near marshes, creeks, ponds, and streams lined with cattails and reeds

White Ibis
Lives near marshes or the coast

Great Horned Owl
Lives in woods, marshes, mountains, and deserts

Greater Yellowlegs
Lives in open marshes and near ponds or streams

Northern Harrier
Lives near marshes, open grasslands, and wet meadows

Norhern Parula
Nests in wet forests and swamps or near ponds

Common Grackle
Lives near parks, farms, woods, and marshes

Red-winged Blackbird
Lives in marshes, swamps, and meadows

Great Blue Heron
Lives near the shallow water of rivers, swamps, and ponds

Black-crowned Night-Heron
Lives in swamps, streams near woods, and near the coast

Barred Owl
Nests in wet woodlands and swamps and along rivers

Wood Duck
Lives near wooded rivers, ponds, and swamps and visits marshes in summer and fall

Swallow-tailed Kite
Prefers marshes, swampy forests, and pine woods

In the swamp

Marshes, wetlands and other humid habitats make a lush and comfortable home for these water-loving birds. Thick trees are perfect for nesting, knobby cypress knees provide perches in the water, and the swamp is full of all kinds of delicious things to eat.

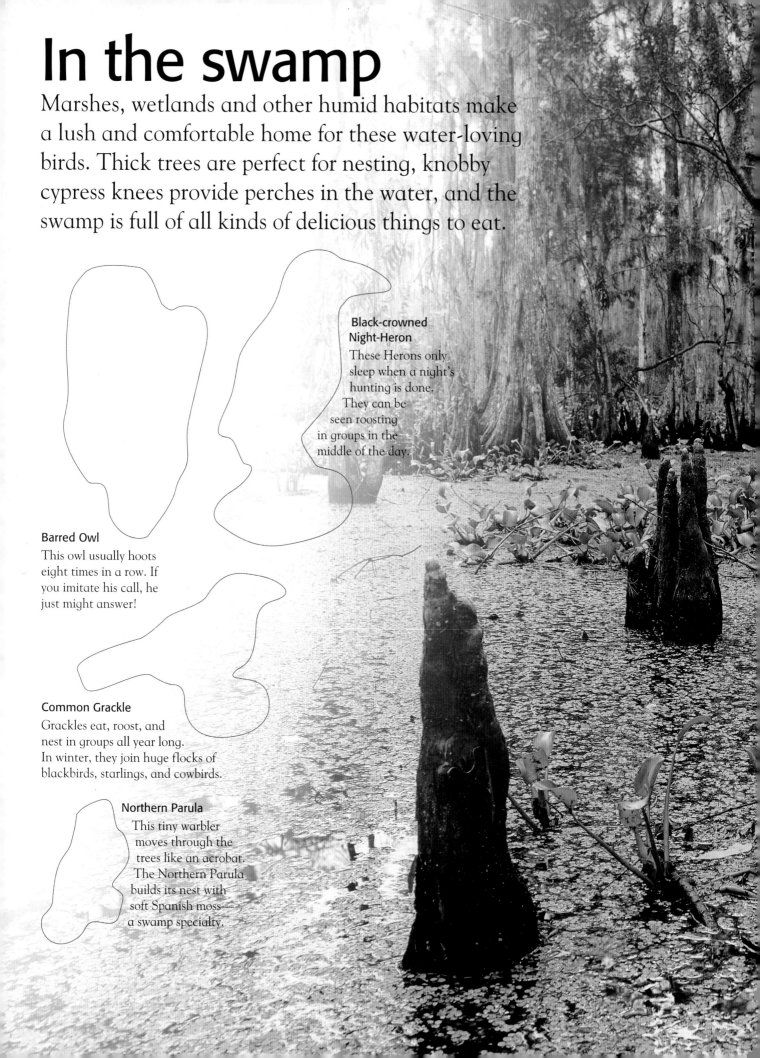

Black-crowned Night-Heron

These Herons only sleep when a night's hunting is done. They can be seen roosting in groups in the middle of the day.

Barred Owl

This owl usually hoots eight times in a row. If you imitate his call, he just might answer!

Common Grackle

Grackles eat, roost, and nest in groups all year long. In winter, they join huge flocks of blackbirds, starlings, and cowbirds.

Northern Parula

This tiny warbler moves through the trees like an acrobat. The Northern Parula builds its nest with soft Spanish moss—a swamp specialty.

In the mountains

After soaring high in the air or hunting for food
on this wooded mountaintop, birds can perch
on the tall trees, rest among the brush,
or drink from the stream
when it's time to rest.

Song Sparrow
This little bird earns
its name by singing for
up to two hours at a time!

Scarlet Tanager
In the fall, the bright red feathers
of the Tanager change to dull green
and yellow. But its wings and tail
stay black throughout the year.